A Peck of Peaches

A Georgia Number Book

Written by Carol Crane and Illustrated by Mark Braught

Text Copyright © 2007 Carol Crane
Illustration Copyright © 2007 Mark Braught

Sleeping Bear Press™

310 North Main Street, Suite 300
Chelsea, MI 48118
www.sleepingbearpress.com

© 2007 Sleeping Bear Press is an imprint of The Gale Group, Inc.

Printed and bound in China.

First Edition

10 9 8 7 6 5 4 3 2 1

Library of Congress Cataloging-in-Publication Data

Crane, Carol, 1933-
A peck of peaches : a Georgia number book / written by Carol Crane;
illustrated by Mark Braught.
p. cm.
Summary: "Using numbers to introduce topics, many of Georgia's famous
people, landmarks, and state symbols are introduced including Martin
Luther King Jr., the nine Greats Lakes of Georgia, loggerhead sea
turtles, and sharks' teeth"—Provided by publisher.
ISBN 978-1-58536-177-9
1. Georgia—Juvenile literature. 2. Counting—Juvenile literature.
I. Braught, Mark. II. Title.

F286.3.C735 2007
975.8—dc22   2007005463

1 is for the SS *Savannah*,
        a paddle wheel churning, a bent smokestack.
    The first steamship to cross the Atlantic,
            puffing smoke that was black.

The SS *Savannah* left Savannah, Georgia with both steam and sails on May 22, 1819. She crossed the ocean on an historic trip that would take her to England, Sweden, Russia, Norway, and Denmark. The ship was 100 feet long and weighed 320 tons. Sails were placed on the ship to navigate in wind. When there was no wind, a wheel with wooden paddles linked by iron chains and powered by steam moved the ship forward.

Black coal smoke came from the smokestack and when the ship approached the Ireland shore, it was thought to be on fire. A ship was sent to rescue all on board, but could not catch up with the SS *Savannah*. The cabin of the ship was decorated elegantly, but to no avail. Since many were afraid of a ship with smoke coming out of its stack and the fire below deck, no one was willing to pay a fare on this new ship. Steamship designer Robert Fulton had successfully sailed steamships on rivers but everyone was afraid to cross the Atlantic on a new venture.

one

1

As the largest wading bird in all of North America, wood storks make their nests in treetops around cypress swamps or mangroves, making Georgia's wetlands a desirable place for wood storks to live. Raccoons are known to eat the tennis-ball-sized eggs of the wood stork. As long as there is water beneath the nest for alligators, they will help keep the raccoons away. The nests are on a huge stick platform usually 3 to 4 feet wide. Colonies of wood storks nest together. The young birds chatter endlessly while the older stork has a dull croak.

The adult birds are white with black flight feathers and tail, long black stilt-like legs, and pink feet. Their dark bills rake back and forth through the marsh water looking for fish, or other prey. When the bill touches a fish, the bill snaps shut very quickly and the bird raises its head skyward and swallows.

The wood stork has been an endangered species but is making a comeback with the help of the U.S. Fish and Wildlife Service.

two
2

Waiting and watching over their nest,
high with the swamp in view.
A treetop home for the little ones,
wood storks fly in as number 2.

Shrimp boats, called trawlers, line the docks of the islands along the Georgia coast. They leave early in the morning and hope to come back heavy with their catch of shrimp in the evening. The boats look as if they have wings when trawling for shrimp. Trawling means to fish using trawl nets, a strong fishing net that drags along the sea bottom. Two horizontal side booms that look like masts are attached to the nets. The trawler lowers the nets, scooping up the shrimp. Large winches are used to lift the heavy nets out of the water.

Shrimp are Georgia's most valuable ocean crop. Each female shrimp releases 500,000 to 1 million eggs into the ocean. After the eggs hatch and grow, the juvenile shrimp feed on bottom algae, small animals, and debris.

When shrimp are served they are pink in color. However, when shrimp are caught they are a dull gray. As heat is applied during cooking, a chemical reaction occurs and the shrimp turn a reddish orange, or pink, color.

three

3

3 shrimp boats are a comin'
chuggin' in from the ocean blue.
Heavy in the water with their catch—
work has just begun for the crew.

Martin Luther King Jr., born in Atlanta, Georgia in 1929, gave his well-known "I have a dream" speech on the steps of the Lincoln Memorial in Washington, D.C. At the age of 35, he was the youngest person awarded the Nobel Peace Prize. He worked for full equality, which means the right to vote, drink from public water fountains, eat in dining rooms, go to good schools, be able to ride school buses, and many other basic civil rights. His voice was heard throughout the world. January 17th has been designated Martin Luther King Day in the United States, honoring this great man.

There are many African Americans with distinguished careers who call Georgia home. Gertrude "Ma" Rainey, the Mother of the Blues, grew up in Georgia and is a member of the Georgia Music Hall of Fame. A United States postal stamp was issued in her honor in 1994. Ray Charles, who was blind, overcame adversity and was considered a pioneer in rhythm and blues. Other musicians, including Little Richard and Gladys Knight, were born in Georgia.

four

4

4 His speech, "I have a dream"—
historic words we know—
There should be justice, it would seem.
Marching forward he did go.

Of our border states we count **5**,
North Carolina, South Carolina, and Tennessee,
Florida and Alabama, too.
Friendly neighbors in this land of the free.

Tennessee

North Carolina

South Carolina

Alabama

Georgia

Florida

Two mighty Appalachian rivers wind along the sides of Georgia. The Savannah River forms the border of South Carolina to the east. The Chattahoochee River separates Georgia from Alabama to the west. Chattahoochee is from the Cherokee Indian words "chatto," a stone, and "hoche," marked or flowered. The river flows downstream from the Blue Ridge Mountains near Brasstown Bald, traveling through Florida to the Gulf of Mexico.

In the north Georgia shares a mountainous border with Tennessee and North Carolina. The Atlantic coastline, with islands and beaches, is to the southeast. Florida is the neighboring state in the south and shares logging, paper, and pulp industries. On the southeastern corner are marshes and the St. Mary's River.

The beautiful Blue Ridge Mountains share a border with Alabama and Tennessee to the north. It is called the "Tag Corner," where Tennessee (T), Alabama (A), and Georgia (G) meet in the northwest corner of the state.

five
5

6 shark teeth,
washed upon our shore.
These fossils are great fun to find.
Oh look! I just found some more.

The shark tooth was designated as the official state fossil in 1976. After a storm or during low tide there are many to be discovered on the beach. Amateur collectors have found the teeth in a variety of colors: black, gray, white, brown, blue, and reddish brown.

Sharks' teeth are set in layered rows in the gums. If one tooth falls out, a tooth from another layer takes its place. A shark may shed as many as 50,000 teeth in its lifetime. Sharks do not have bones like ours. Their skeleton is made up of the same material our nose and ears are made of, cartilage.

Black tip, bull shark, hammerhead, and lemon are just a few of the many different species of shark found along Georgia's shores. The warm spring waters around Cumberland Island are believed to be the largest shark breeding grounds on the East coast. Shark attacks are not common, but do happen. Always observe the shark warnings posted along the shores of swimming areas.

six

6

Visitors are amazed at the breathtaking colors of Georgia's Little Grand Canyon in Providence Canyon State Park. In the 1800s farmers cut down trees and eliminated vegetation. Heavy thunderstorms soon eroded the farmland. Little ditches became big holes and gullies. Vast amounts of sand and silt washed down into the Chattahoochee River. Farmers were even losing cattle and farm equipment over the canyon rim. As years went by, big chunks of earth fell from the steep-sided walls into the canyons, forming gorges which today are 150 feet deep from rim to bottom, a half mile long, and 300 feet across.

The layers of rock and sand range in color from tan, salmon, shades of pink, orange, hues of purple, and white. This act of nature caused by poor farming practices years ago has created a beautiful work of art. The Red Blaze Trail is seven miles around the rim of the canyon. There is also a three-mile trail called White Blaze where you can explore nine fingerlike canyons and see wildflowers and the rare plum leaf azalea.

seven

7

In the "Little Grand Canyon"
colored sand and rocks are what we see.
7 hikers on the trail,
there's not a better place to be.

Georgia was fortunate to host the G-8 summit meeting at Sea Island in June of 2004. G-8 (Group of 8) includes eight major industrial nations whose representatives come together to discuss issues facing the world and its environment. The sea turtles nesting on Georgia's beaches during the summit meeting made participants aware of this threatened species.

More than 1,200 elementary schoolchildren in Georgia submitted names for the sea turtles in honor of the countries participating in the G-8 summit. The students learned about each of the countries in the G-8 and submitted the following winning names for the turtles:

U.S. / *Cherokee Rose* / Wildflower
France / *Bon Jour* / Good Morning
Germany / *Ormanda* / Of the sea
Japan / *Oki* / Open sea
United Kingdom / *Tea Cake*
Italy / *Bellissima* / Most Beautiful
Canada / *Aurora* / Northern Lights
Russia / *Cherepakha* / Turtle

eight

8

A worldwide plan
to affect the sea turtles' fate.
Children joining the project.
Loggerheads become our 8.

Each of these great lakes was created by the United States Army Corps of Engineers. These lakes are not naturally occurring and have been man-made by channeling rivers and constructing dams and reservoirs. The result is power generation, navigation, and flood control. Almost every lake in Georgia is man-made. Landforms with inadequate slope conditions and geological conditions prevented natural lakes from being formed.

One of the most interesting of the nine lakes is Carters Lake, where water flows down pipes from the mountain to generate power all day. At night, the huge pumps send the water back up to the lake to be used the next day. This is one of the few reverse dams in the United States. Clarks Hill Lake is one of the largest inland bodies of water in the South.

nine

9

9 Great Lakes of Georgia
created in the north, south, east, and west.
Each one unique
make swimming, boating, and fishing the best.

Margaret Mitchell (Martha) was born in 1900 in Atlanta, Georgia. One day she came home and announced she was not going back to school because she hated arithmetic. In an effort to show Martha the importance of education, her mother showed her the ruined plantations and the effects of the Civil War. This so impressed young Martha that she went back to school the next day and conquered math.

Martha wrote many stories as a child and worked for a magazine as an adult; however, her most important story was one of the Civil War—*Gone with the Wind*. It took her ten years to write this epic novel, which received the Pulitzer Prize in 1937. More than 30 million copies were sold in six months.

She was such an avid reader that her husband could not find any new books for her to read in the Atlanta Public Library. He bought her a typewriter and challenged her to write her own stories.

ten
10

From a novel, *Gone with the Wind*,
dressed in layers and lace are 10 Southern belles,
part of Georgia's history from long ago.
Can you imagine the Civil War tale it tells?

The state of Georgia has many ties to farming where peaches, peanuts, onions, and cane sugar are cultivated. Growing cane sugar is an old family tradition in some areas. During Thanksgiving time the air can be sweet with the smell of cane syrup cooking.

The cane is planted in early spring and cut in the fall. Cane grows in round stalks sometimes 10 feet tall. The leaves are cut down at ground level. The cane is taken to the sugar mill where the juice is pressed out by large rollers called crushers. Some farmers still use mules to operate the rollers but today most are run by electricity. The long stalks of cane are fed into the presses, and sweet juices come gushing out. Then the juice is put into a large cast iron pot and cooked off into syrup. Finding a bottle of cane syrup at a breakfast table, sopping up the sweetness with a biscuit, or drizzling syrup on pancakes is mouth-wateringly good.

eleven
11

11 bottles of syrup
pressed from fields of cane we grew.
Grannie says "Come try it"
on biscuits, cornbread, and pancakes too.

Settlers have always needed a way to cross streams and rivers. At first they laid logs across the water, but as more people needed to cross with wagons and goods, bridges became a necessity. One of the most prominent builders of covered bridges in Georgia was Horace King (1807-1885). He was a slave who became one of the most talented bridge builders in the South.

He worked with John Godwin, who later granted him his freedom. Before the Civil War a slave master could not simply free his slaves. King and Godwin traveled to Ohio and there he was formally freed under Ohio law.

Covered bridges are historic monuments from the 1800s. They are a reminder of the people who labored without modern electrical tools, and with ingenuity constructed wooden tunnels for the settlers who came to Georgia. The Georgia Department of Transportation notes there are many covered bridges in Georgia but just 12 qualify as historic, and many have required extensive care.

twelve
12

12 historic covered bridges,
a vision of our state's past.
Transporting settlers over streams and rivers,
builder's designs unsurpassed.

There were twelve colonies settled in North America and flourishing. Then 50 years later Georgia, the last of the famous thirteen, became part of this. These thirteen colonies rebelled against the Royal Crown. They signed the Declaration of Independence in 1776, becoming independent of England. This established the United States of America. The founder of Georgia, James Oglethorpe, saw all thirteen colonies become an independent nation after the Revolutionary War.

The National Museum of Patriotism in Atlanta opened its doors on July 4, 2004. A replica of the Liberty Bell, one of the historic symbols on display, was rung thirteen times. It represented the thirteen colonies and most importantly, Georgia. Visitors can ring the Liberty Bell replica, learn from a sculpture of the Statue of Liberty, and watch a stirring film on the meaning of patriotism.

thirteen
13

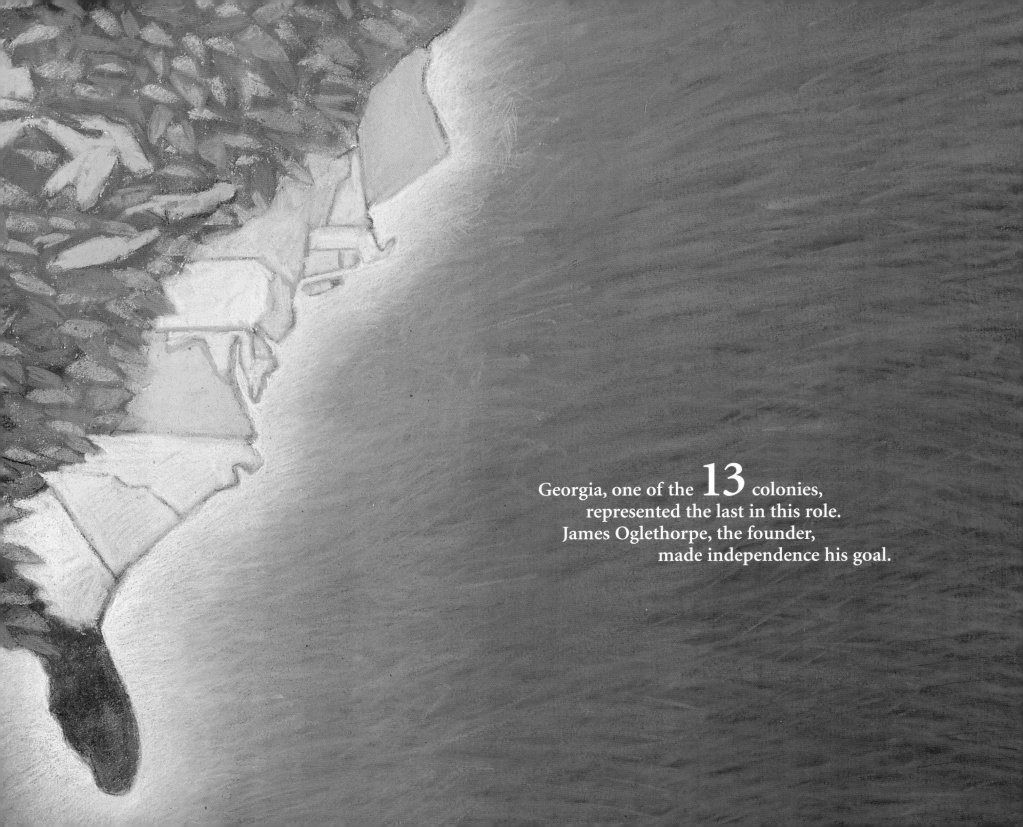

Georgia, one of the **13** colonies,
represented the last in this role.
James Oglethorpe, the founder,
made independence his goal.

The pine tar and pitch from pine trees was used for waterproofing the hulls of the first wooden ships. It was also used for paint thinner, roofing cement, soap, candy, medicines, and insecticides. Turpentine mills were once common in Georgia. In the mills, the pine resin was heated and turpentine was produced from the vapor. The spicy smell of the pine tree pitch was very strong.

The resin was collected by chopping into the bark of the tree trunks. Two metal pieces were placed into the slash made by the axe that formed a V-shaped funnel. Then a nail was driven into the bark and a cup of either pottery or metal was put on the nail for the resin to drip into.

Many of the trees died after being cut into and the pine tar drained from them. As more families moved into Georgia, land was needed for farms, causing many turpentine mills to close. However, you can still see some of the notches and cups that were left on the trees by this industry.

fourteen
14

14 tall pine trees,
standing like soldiers in a row.
Gentle winds make them sway
with musical motion to and fro.

Opossums are the only marsupial found in the United States. The mother carries her young in a pouch like the Australian kangaroo. The babies are the size of a honeybee when born, and live in their mother's pouch drinking her milk for three months. Fossils of the opossum have been found dating back 70 million years. Just think, these little animals lived during the Age of the Dinosaurs!

The opossum is a garbage collector and will clean up crumbs and dog or cat food that is left out in the open. They also love to eat insects, snails, rodents, berries, and vegetables. They are nature's environmental engineers cleaning up garbage from our forests and streambeds. They use their tails to balance when climbing up trees.

A cartoon character named Pogo 'Possum created by Walt Kelly was known to reside in the Okefenokee Swamp. Georgia's general assembly voted Pogo the State 'Possum in 1992.

fifteen
15

15 is for Georgia's creeping opossums
each day learning different ways.
North America's only marsupial
eating, growing, and playing for days and days.

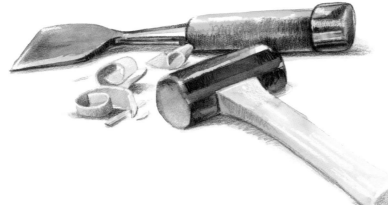

20 log cabins built at Foxfire,
an Appalachian project of writing.
Students interviewing their families,
creating a magazine so rich and inviting.

Foxfire: An eerie blue-green glow found in forests which often comes from mushrooms that grow on decaying logs. Students in Georgia started a project, named Foxfire, of interviewing relatives and neighbors about living in the mountains. Stepping back in time, they told what life was like long ago.

The information the students gathered documented the history, culture, and language while teaching creative writing and communication. In 1972 the first book, *The Foxfire Book*, was published. Since then, eleven *Foxfire* books have been widely read and used.

Foxfire book sales have helped to buy land and fund the construction of 20 log structures and the Foxfire Museum in Mountain City, Georgia. There is an 1820 one-room home, an animal barn, a replica of a chapel, and a gristmill. Also on display is the only existing wagon known to have been used on the Trail of Tears.

twenty
20

Brunswick, Georgia claims to be the place of origin for Brunswick stew. However, many other states with towns named Brunswick lay claim to this 1800s dish. A visitor center near Brunswick has a plaque and huge iron pot weighing 25 pounds. This huge vessel greets you and claims to be the original favorite Southern dish recipe location.

During settler days, wild game such as squirrel, deer, rabbit, or bear were the available stew meats. For variety corn and squash were put into the pot for flavor. The southeast Native Americans knew how to cook in huge pots made of earthenware before any pioneers came to the area. Today there are a variety of recipes for this tasty stew: Five pounds of either beef, chicken, or pork with five pounds of onions, five pounds of potatoes, five pounds of tomatoes, and five pounds of parsnips. Have you ever made stew?

twenty-five

25

10 potatoes, 10 tomatoes, and 5 onions make our **25**.
In a huge kettle, ready to greet you,
Brunswick, Georgia is the place
that claims the origin of this stew.

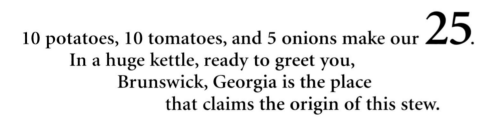

You can grow a birdhouse right in your own backyard! Native Americans grew gourds for eating but found purple martins would use the shell as a house, and the birds would take care of the pesky mosquitoes.

Try planting gourd seeds and watch the vines flower and turn into bottle gourds. Ten to twelve gourds will grow on every vine. The vines get heavy, so if you drape them over a fence or trellis the gourds will not be flat on one side from lying on the ground.

In the fall the gourds are harvested. Scrape out the seeds and wash and dry out the inside. Drill a hole large enough for the birds to get into their new home. Drill two small holes in the bottom of the bottle gourd for drainage. Drill two holes in the top, and thread a cord through the holes for hanging up your birdhouse. Decorating the gourd can be fun, and be sure to varnish the outside to prevent it from getting moldy when hung outdoors.

30 Georgia bottle gourds
hanging on a garden line.
Made into martin houses,
where birds can live and dine.

40 is for the mountain children
who came to hear Martha Berry.
They called her the "Sunday Lady,"
and her school became legendary.

On a Sunday, Martha was sitting in a small log cabin reading Bible stories. Three mountain children from Possum Trot sat down and listened. The next Sunday more children came—brothers, sisters, and even the dog. They were starved for learning, and loved hearing her stories.

This was the beginning of her mission to teach children. Attendance in her school was growing but it was not enough for the "Sunday Lady." She needed dormitories and buildings so boys would be able to attend school on a regular basis. Martha Berry, through hard work and donated time and money, established a school for boys.

She taught her students not only how to read and write but how to wash clothes, work a garden, cook, and build a house. In 1902 the Boy's Industrial School was founded and in 1909, the Martha Berry School for Girls opened. These schools were the beginning of what is known today as Berry College.

Built to look like a modern Noah's Ark, the Georgia Aquarium in Atlanta is considered "the world's largest aquarium." Since its doors opened in November, 2000 visitors enter with expectations of seeing something grand, and they do! The blue metal and glass ark looks like it is sailing through ocean waves. The ship's hull appears to emerge from two large buildings having roofs that were designed to look like ocean swells.

Exhibits include touch tanks where rays and sharks swim by and you may touch their smooth bodies. Imagine looking up to an overhead river to see North American fish from the bottom up. In the Cold Water Quest exhibit you'll be in awe of Beluga whales, California sea lions, and African black-footed penguins. The aquarium has almost 8 million gallons of water, where close to 100,000 animals live.

The Georgia Aquarium is currently home to three whale sharks and is the only aquarium outside Asia to provide a home for this fish—the largest fish in the world.

fifty
50

50 children and their teachers
on a school field trip,
waiting to enter the aquarium
designed like a glass ship.

100 is for tarpons and also for
the miles of Georgia coastline
where these huge fish were rescued,
now viewed rain or shine.

Tarpon can weigh up to 300 pounds. They are called silver kings because they have large silver scales, which give a bright flash when jumping into the air. Often tarpon are seen on the ocean waves where they roll and gulp air in oxygen-rich waters. Tarpon often swim close to shore looking for warmer waters during the cold winter months. Near Skidaway Island 100 tarpon were stranded off the Georgia coast in a tidal pool. The Georgia Aquarium rescued these fish.

Georgia has approximately 100 miles of shoreline on the Atlantic Ocean. One hundred miles of salt water marshes with windswept grass waving in the ocean breeze, barrier islands, sandy beaches, and tidal pools.

Even though Georgia's coast is small in comparison to the rest of the state it is indeed a magical place. The colored hues of their sunrise and sunset look like baskets of fresh orange-pink-yellow peaches.

one hundred

100

Carol Crane

Carol Crane is an historian and author who has always been a journal writer. Traveling around the country, she speaks at reading conventions and schools, inspiring children and educators on the fabric that makes up the quilt of this great country. Her greatest joy is to have a child say, "Wow! I didn't know that."

In addition to *A Peck of Peaches*, she has also written books about China, Florida, Texas, Alaska, Georgia, South Carolina, North Carolina, Alabama, and Delaware; and number books for South Carolina, North Carolina, Florida, and Texas. She is also the author of *P is for Pilgrim: A Thanksgiving Alphabet*.

Mark Braught

Mark Braught's 27 years of professional experience have earned him prestigious awards from the American Advertising Federation (ADDY), *Communication Arts*, the NY Art Directors Club, and the Society of Illustrators among others. He received his degree in graphic design from Indiana State University, and attended the Minneapolis College of Art & Design. He lives in Commerce, Georgia, with his wife Laura, their five cats, and Charlie the dog.

He also illustrated the companion alphabet title: *P is for Peach: A Georgia Alphabet*, along with *T is for Touchdown: A Football Alphabet*; *J is for Jump Shot: A Basketball Alphabet*; and *Cosmo's Moon*, all published by Sleeping Bear Press.